KT-102-744

November 1992

Deine Marlis

·THE LITTLE SCENTED LIBRARY·

LAVENDER

·JOANNA SHEEN·

DORLING KINDERSLEY

LONDON • NEW YORK • STUTTGART

A DORLING KINDERSLEY BOOK

•

SERIES EDITORS HEATHER DEWHURST, MARY LAMBERT
PROJECT EDITOR SUSAN THOMPSON
ART EDITOR CAROL McCLEEVE
MANAGING EDITOR JANE LAING
SENIOR ART EDITOR DAVID ROBINSON
PRODUCTION MERYL SILBERT
PHOTOGRAPHY MATTHEW WARD

•

FIRST PUBLISHED IN GREAT BRITAIN IN 1991
BY DORLING KINDERSLEY LIMITED,
9 HENRIETTA STREET, LONDON WC2E 8PS

•

A CIP CATALOGUE RECORD FOR THIS BOOK IS AVAILABLE FROM THE BRITISH LIBRARY

ISBN 0-86318-562-2

•

COMPUTER PAGE MAKE-UP BY THE COOLING BROWN PARTNERSHIP
REPRODUCED BY COLOURSCAN, SINGAPORE
PRINTED IN HONG KONG

2

Contents

INTRODUCTION

A LUXURIOUS HAZE of purple lavender is one of life's more simple pleasures. Along with the heady scents of old-fashioned roses, honeysuckle, and freshly mown grass, the sweet fragrance of lavender transports me immediately to the long, dreamy summers of my childhood.

Lavender has long been popular. Both Queen Elizabeth and Queen Victoria used it as a conserve and perfume, and tradition has it that on Midsummer's Eve, revellers throw bunches of lavender on to bonfires as part of the ritual celebrations. Lavender is also an important healing herb and is still used today in aromatherapy to ease tension and headaches.

Dried lavender is a main ingredient in many pot-pourri recipes and is frequently used to fill sachets, cushions, and herb pillows; lavender can even be used in cooking. Fresh lavender adds a decorative element to flower displays, and its scent perfumes any bouquet. Lavender oil can be used in moisturizers, skin toners, creams, perfumes, and bath oils.

There are many ways to enjoy the wonderful scent of lavender. When its flowering season is over, let the fragrance of lavender linger on with the ideas suggested in this little book.

THE SCENT OF LAVENDER

L AVENDER OIL IS AN ESSENTIAL OIL frequently used in aromatherapy massage to relieve nervous tension and aches. It is first mixed with a vegetable oil – a carrier – in the ratio of six drops of essential oil to every 50 g (2 oz) of carrier oil. Suitable carrier oils include: safflower, soybean, sesame, and sunflower oil. Other essential oils frequently used in aromatherapy include lemon and rosemary oils.

Carrier oil

Vetiver oil

Lavender oil

LAVENDER OIL
Lavender oil is distilled from the plant and is then mixed with a carrier oil for use in aromatherapy massage.

Lemon

SOOTHING SOLUTIONS

Anxiety and nervous tension can be relieved simply by adding a few drops of neat lavender and vetiver oil in a hot, relaxing bath; or try gently massaging the stomach area with a mixture of lavender oil and a carrier oil. For aching feet that have done a lot of walking, a restorative ten-minute soak in a bowl of water containing several drops each of lavender and juniper oils works wonders. For fast relief from sunburn, add 20 drops of lavender and chamomile oils to a cool bath.

MEDICINAL REMEDIES

To relieve headaches, add 12 drops of lavender oil to 100 g (4 oz) of carrier oil and massage gently around the temples and the base of the skull. To help restore the balance of the nervous system, use 6 drops each of cypress and lavender oils in 100 g (4 oz) carrier oil; massage the stomach area in an anticlockwise direction with your right hand. Lavender oil is also useful for insect bites and stings; a drop on an insect bite will soothe and protect against infection.

Carrier oil

Lavender oil

Lavender

Rosemary

USING LAVENDER

*L*AVENDER HAS MANY DECORATIVE and aromatic uses inside the home. One simple yet stunning idea is to pack a plain basket or pot with several large bunches of fresh lavender and display it in a prominent position in the hall or living room. Less extravagant but no less charming arrangements can be created using small sprigs of lavender in combination with other small, scented flowers.

To preserve lavender's summery scent throughout the winter, hang bunches up to dry and then fill sachets and cushions with the dried lavender.

BASKET DISPLAY

This breath-taking display will form the centrepiece in any room. Fill a basket with a dried foam block and insert bunches of lavender into this until the basket virtually overflows. Add ribbon bows to finish.

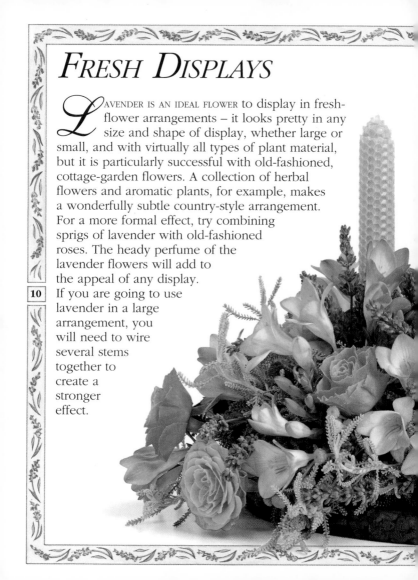

FRESH DISPLAYS

*L*AVENDER IS AN IDEAL FLOWER to display in fresh-flower arrangements – it looks pretty in any size and shape of display, whether large or small, and with virtually all types of plant material, but it is particularly successful with old-fashioned, cottage-garden flowers. A collection of herbal flowers and aromatic plants, for example, makes a wonderfully subtle country-style arrangement. For a more formal effect, try combining sprigs of lavender with old-fashioned roses. The heady perfume of the lavender flowers will add to the appeal of any display. If you are going to use lavender in a large arrangement, you will need to wire several stems together to create a stronger effect.

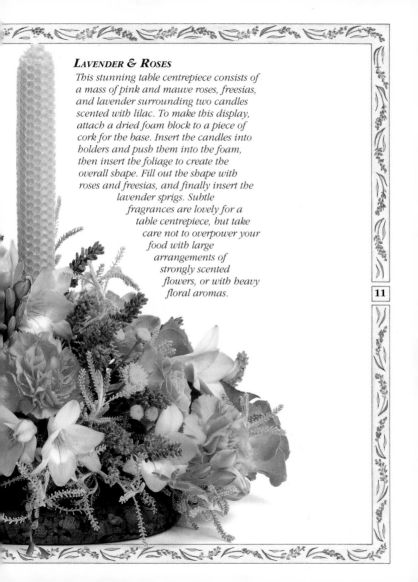

LAVENDER & ROSES

This stunning table centrepiece consists of a mass of pink and mauve roses, freesias, and lavender surrounding two candles scented with lilac. To make this display, attach a dried foam block to a piece of cork for the base. Insert the candles into holders and push them into the foam, then insert the foliage to create the overall shape. Fill out the shape with roses and freesias, and finally insert the lavender sprigs. Subtle fragrances are lovely for a table centrepiece, but take care not to overpower your food with large arrangements of strongly scented flowers, or with heavy floral aromas.

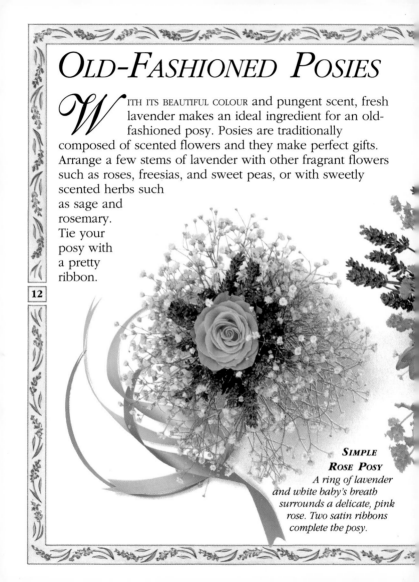

OLD-FASHIONED POSIES

*W*ITH ITS BEAUTIFUL COLOUR and pungent scent, fresh lavender makes an ideal ingredient for an old-fashioned posy. Posies are traditionally composed of scented flowers and they make perfect gifts. Arrange a few stems of lavender with other fragrant flowers such as roses, freesias, and sweet peas, or with sweetly scented herbs such as sage and rosemary. Tie your posy with a pretty ribbon.

12

SIMPLE ROSE POSY
A ring of lavender and white baby's breath surrounds a delicate, pink rose. Two satin ribbons complete the posy.

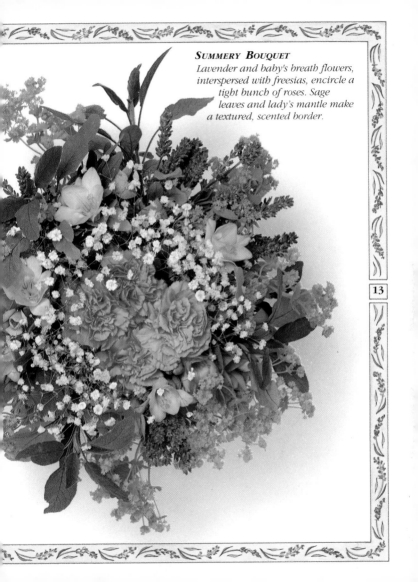

SUMMERY BOUQUET
Lavender and baby's breath flowers, interspersed with freesias, encircle a tight bunch of roses. Sage leaves and lady's mantle make a textured, scented border.

13

DRIED DISPLAYS

*L*AVENDER IS AN IDEAL FLOWER to use in a dried-flower arrangement as it dries so easily, and it has the added appeal of retaining its wonderfully rich scent. To air-dry lavender, simply hang a bunch upside-down in a warm, dry area for about a week. For a stunning yet simple display, group several bunches of dried lavender in a rustic container, or try combining it with dried peonies, roses, and herbs for a more complex arrangement.

SIMPLE & EFFECTIVE
The beauty of this flower arrangement (below) is in its simplicity. A cluster of dried peach-coloured roses nestles in a small glass dish, surrounded by a fragrant frill of lavender and a few achillea flower heads.

FLOWERS IN A TEACUP
This pretty little teacup (above) makes the perfect setting for an arrangement of dried lavender, red spray carnations, and achillea flowers.

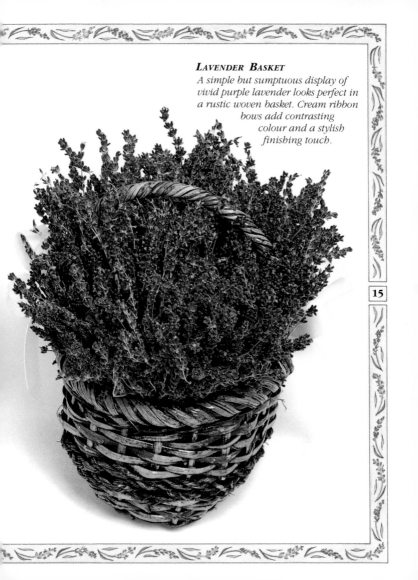

LAVENDER BASKET

A simple but sumptuous display of vivid purple lavender looks perfect in a rustic woven basket. Cream ribbon bows add contrasting colour and a stylish finishing touch.

TUSSIE MUSSIES

*P*OSIES OF FRESH or dried flowers, or tussie mussies as they were known in the past, make a special token of affection or a thoughtful way to say thank you. Whether they convey a traditional message using the language of flowers, or please the recipient with their colours and fragrance, tussie mussies always make lovely gifts.

CHILD'S ROSE POSY
This posy is made with lavender, masterwort and roses.

FORMAL BOUQUET
The loops of satin ribbon add style to this large posy of scented flowers.

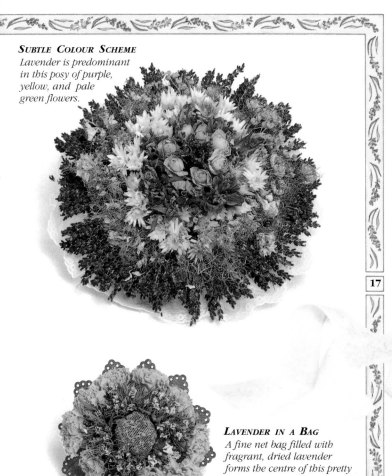

SUBTLE COLOUR SCHEME
Lavender is predominant in this posy of purple, yellow, and pale green flowers.

17

LAVENDER IN A BAG
A fine net bag filled with fragrant, dried lavender forms the centre of this pretty tussie mussie, and is surrounded by circles of sweet William flowers and golden-coloured carnations.

LAVENDER BUNDLES

L AVENDER BUNDLES are dried stems of lavender woven together with ribbon. They are easy to make, requiring nothing more than a little care, patience, and nimble fingers. Collect the lavender just as it begins to flower so that the flower oils are at their strongest and cut the stems as long as possible. You need 11 or 13 stems for each bundle.

MAKING A LAVENDER BUNDLE

1 Trim the stems of the lavender and tie them all together in a neat bunch, just below the flower heads, with a long piece of narrow ribbon.

2 Gently and carefully bend each stalk back over the flower heads to form a cage around the flowers. If any of the stalks snap, just begin again.

3 Attach a tiny safety pin to the end of the ribbon then weave the ribbon in and out of the stalks, starting at the top and continuing until you reach the base of the flower heads.

4 Wind the ribbon around the stalks of the lavender and tie it in a bow. Trim the stalks to neaten.

COMPLETED BUNDLES

Place the finished lavender bundles in a warm, dark place, such as an airing cupboard, to dry completely before using. Then place them on your dressing table or tuck them in a drawer and enjoy their fragrance.

LAVENDER & LINEN

*L*AVENDER HAS A WONDERFUL FRAGRANCE for scenting all your linens, smelling crisp yet wonderfully warm and clean. Sheets and table linen scented with lavender have been enjoyed by people for literally hundreds of years. Lavender bundles provide both an attractive and practical way to tuck lavender into drawers and linen cupboards. They can also be placed between stored woollen blankets.

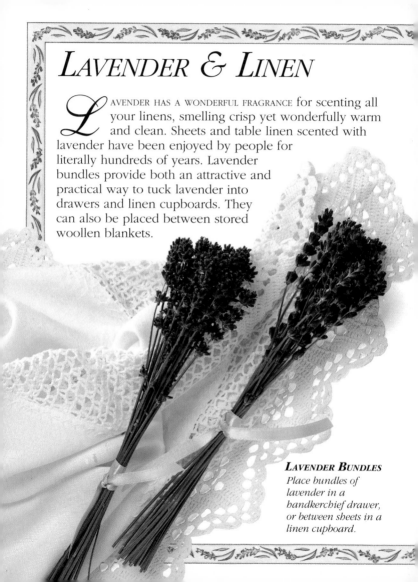

LAVENDER BUNDLES
Place bundles of lavender in a handkerchief drawer, or between sheets in a linen cupboard.

SWEET-SCENTED NAPKINS

Store your linen table napkins by rolling them up with a lavender bundle and securing with a napkin ring. This will give them a fresh, sweet fragrance when you come to use them at the table.

POT POURRIS

*M*AKING YOUR OWN MIX of pot pourri is fun and so rewarding, but also quite easy. All recipes use different combinations of fragrant flowers, but lavender is one of the most popular. Add it to pungent herbs, exotic spices, fixatives and aromatic essential oils.

LAVENDER MIX

Combine lavender flowers and stalks with dried rue leaves and add 6 drops of lavender oil. Decorate with shells.

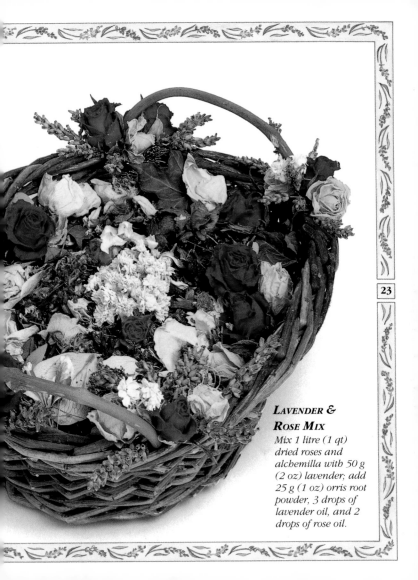

LAVENDER &
ROSE MIX

*Mix 1 litre (1 qt)
dried roses and
alchemilla with 50 g
(2 oz) lavender; add
25 g (1 oz) orris root
powder, 3 drops of
lavender oil, and 2
drops of rose oil.*

EXOTIC POT POURRIS

*W*ITH THE MANY ESSENTIAL oils available today, it is simple to create more exotic pot pourris. Add a few drops of patchouli oil or ylang-ylang oil for a heady fragrance, or mix in some scented woods, such as sandalwood and cedarwood for a musky perfume. In the pot-pourri mix below, a spicy perfume is achieved by using cinnamon, cloves, and nutmegs as well as lavender and orange oils.

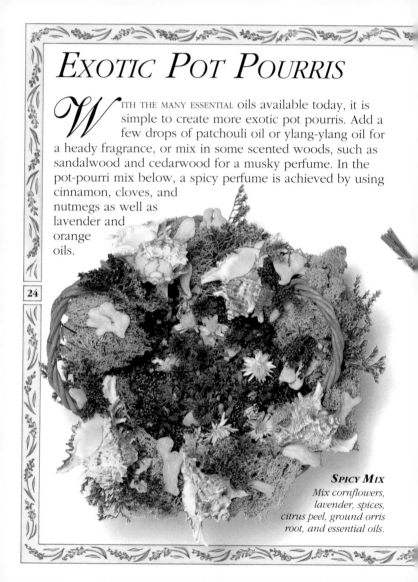

SPICY MIX
Mix cornflowers, lavender, spices, citrus peel, ground orris root, and essential oils.

OLD-FASHIONED ROSE MIX
Mix together 1 litre (1 qt) of dark rose petals and lavender flowers, then add 2 drops each of rose oil and cinnamon oil, and 25 g (1 oz) ground orris root for a fragrant pot-pourri mix (above).

SCENTED BOX
Create an unusual pot pourri (left) by displaying aromatic bay leaves, star anise, cinnamon, and lavender in a compartmented box. Add a few drops of essential oil to strengthen their individual fragrances.

MAKING A SACHET

*L*AVENDER'S CRISP FRAGRANCE has long been popular in scenting laundry. In the past, women draped newly washed linen over aromatic lavender bushes to add a lovely perfume as it dried. Sweet bags or sachets of lavender and other herbs can be tucked between sheets in the linen cupboard to keep the laundry smelling fresh, or tied with ribbon loops and hung from a radiator or drawer handle to perfume the room with the sweet, fresh smell of lavender.

MAKING A LAVENDER SACHET

1 Cut a piece of fabric about 20 x 15 cm (8 x 6 in) and a length of lace 20 cm (8 in) long.

2 Turn under a small hem on one of the long sides and attach the lace to this. Fold the material in half, right sides together, and sew across the bottom and open side. Turn the sachet right-side out and fill it two-thirds full with lavender. Tie a satin ribbon bow around the sachet to seal it.

COMPLEMENTARY COLOURS
Scented sachets made in pretty matching fabric look attractive displayed together. Tie on extra ribbon loops to hang the sachets from a radiator or coat hanger, or place them flat in a drawer or on the dressing table.

PILLOWS

HERBAL PILLOWS have such a wonderful scent that even if they are not guaranteed to be sleep-inducing, their relaxing fragrance can be appreciated at any time of the day. Stuff your pillows with wadding and then add dried lavender, on its own or with other aromatic herbs.

28

DRAWER FRESHENERS
Place small sachets in drawers for a refreshing lavender scent.

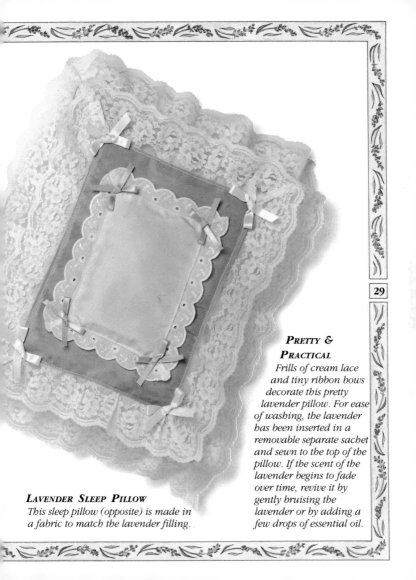

29

PRETTY & PRACTICAL

Frills of cream lace and tiny ribbon bows decorate this pretty lavender pillow. For ease of washing, the lavender has been inserted in a removable separate sachet and sewn to the top of the pillow. If the scent of the lavender begins to fade over time, revive it by gently bruising the lavender or by adding a few drops of essential oil.

LAVENDER SLEEP PILLOW

This sleep pillow (opposite) is made in a fabric to match the lavender filling.

BATH BAGS

*E*NJOY THE SOOTHING FRAGRANCE of lavender in the bathroom with lavender bath bags and pot pourri. Bath bags are easy to make and can be re-used several times. Cut a piece of muslin about 17 cm (7 in) square, and fill the middle with lavender flowers. Gather the edges together and tie them in a bundle. Hang the bag from the hot tap with a ribbon.

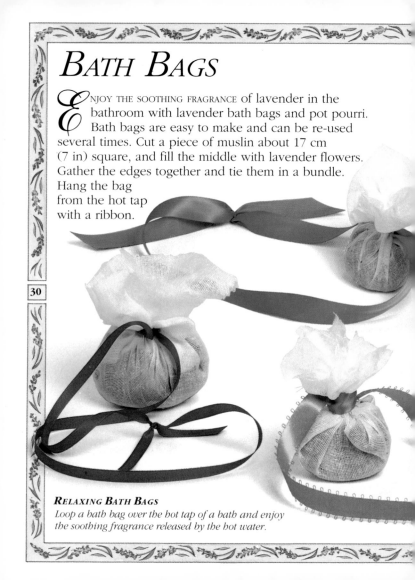

RELAXING BATH BAGS
Loop a bath bag over the hot tap of a bath and enjoy the soothing fragrance released by the hot water.

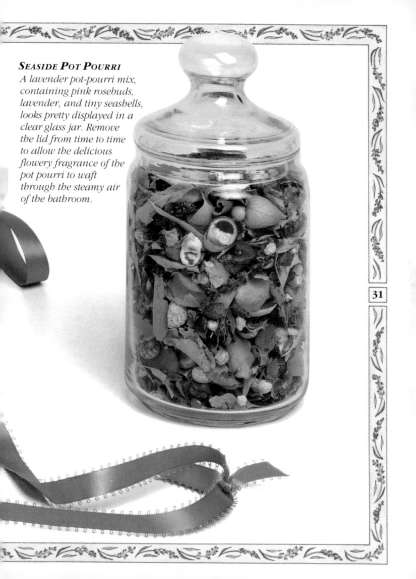

SEASIDE POT POURRI

*A lavender pot-pourri mix,
containing pink rosebuds,
lavender, and tiny seashells,
looks pretty displayed in a
clear glass jar. Remove
the lid from time to time
to allow the delicious
flowery fragrance of the
pot pourri to waft
through the steamy air
of the bathroom.*

31

Bath Oils & Waters

*I*N DAYS GONE BY, large houses had a still-room where the mistress of the house concocted all her aromatic and herbal remedies. Strongly scented lavender makes wonderfully fragrant waters and essences that are perfect for giving as presents. Spend some time searching for just the right bottle for your preparations – antique shops and markets often yield treasures. If you wish to heighten the lavender colour, add a little natural food colouring.

SKIN TONER

Mix together 250 ml (4 fl oz) of lavender flowers and 60 ml (1 fl oz) of ethyl alcohol in a screw-top jar (far left). Leave to steep for six days, shaking daily. Strain and decant.

FACIAL RINSE

Add 7 drops of lavender oil to 500 ml (1 pt) of still mineral water (left).

LAVENDER MOISTURIZER

This concoction (below) makes your skin feel wonderfully smooth and the fragrance is heavenly. In a blender, combine 3 tablespoons each of gum arabic powder and almond oil, and 15 to 20 drops of lavender oil. Turn the blender on to high speed and, while the ingredients are mixing, slowly pour in 300 ml (¹/2 pt) of still mineral water to produce a creamy emulsion. Transfer the moisturizer to a pretty pot and store in the refrigerator.

LAVENDER & ROSE CASTING BOTTLE

Pour 200 ml (8 fl oz) of rose water into a bottle (left). Add 3 drops of lavender oil and 3 sprigs of fresh rosemary. Seal the bottle and leave it in a warm place, such as an airing cupboard, for a couple of weeks for the scents to infuse. Then strain and decant into a decorative bottle. Sprinkle this water on to linen as you iron it for a lovely, lingering perfume.

BATH OIL

In a jar (right), mix 125 ml (5 fl oz) almond oil and 5 tablespoons of lavender oil. Cover; leave for two weeks.

PERFUMED SOAPS

*S*OAPS OFTEN HAVE AN ATTRACTIVE FRAGRANCE of their own but, if you like, you can perfume plain, unscented soaps with a refreshing scent of lavender. Simply place the soaps in a container of lavender pot pourri and leave for a week or two. As well as looking charming, this is a lovely way to present guest soaps.

SOAPS IN A BASKET
A charming basket decorated with roses makes a delightful container for lavender soaps, which are embedded in lavender flowers.

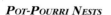

POT-POURRI NESTS

Pretty pink guest soaps nestle in a bed of richly scented eucalyptus, peony, and lavender pot pourri inside two old-fashioned glass dishes.

BATHROOM FEATURE

Pretty glass dishes are particularly attractive as containers for pot pourri and soap, as you can see the colourful ingredients through the sides, adding to the effect of the display. Another decorative idea for a container would be to use a rustic basket lined with a lace-edged handkerchief. Decorate all the visible sides of your pot pourri with beautifully shaped and colourful petals, so that it looks as wonderful as it smells!

A TASTE OF LAVENDER

ALTHOUGH MAINLY PRODUCED FOR ITS PERFUME, lavender lends a delicious and elusive flavour to food, both sweet and savoury. In cooked dishes, add one or two leaf shoots to casseroles and remove before serving. A sprig of lavender shoots enhances roast lamb in a similar way to rosemary. Apple jelly made with a sprig of lavender is especially successful with pork and lamb, while lavender-flavoured mustard provides a delicious accompaniment to beef and veal. Fresh lavender shoots also add a pungent flavour to summer salads.

Lavender also blends well with sweet dishes. Try adding the flowers to ice-creams, sorbets, and even fresh fruit salads for refreshing and tasty desserts. For a truly delicious pudding, stew apples with a few lavender flowers and serve with whipped cream.

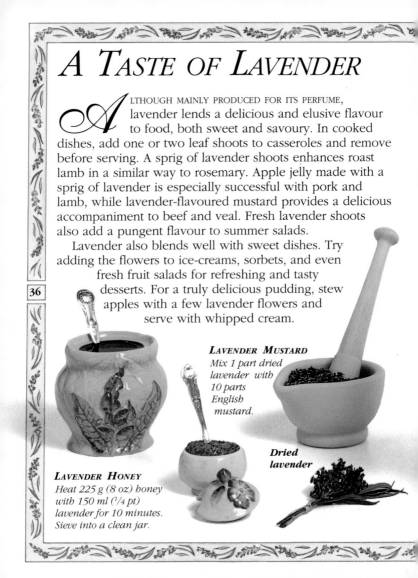

LAVENDER MUSTARD
Mix 1 part dried lavender with 10 parts English mustard.

Dried lavender

LAVENDER HONEY
Heat 225 g (8 oz) honey with 150 ml (¼ pt) lavender for 10 minutes. Sieve into a clean jar.

LAVENDER OIL
Insert 2 or 3 sprigs of fresh lavender in a bottle of virgin olive oil and leave to mature in the sun for two weeks. It adds a fresh taste to salads.

LAVENDER VINEGARS
Insert several sprigs of fresh lavender into a bottle of white wine vinegar or cider vinegar, then seal the bottle and leave it for two to three weeks in a warm or sunny spot. Use the vinegars to add a sharp flavour to savoury sauces, salad dressings, and lavender jellies.

37

TEA TIME

*L*AVENDER TEA HAS LONG BEEN a remedy for headaches caused by tension and nervous problems, and was even popular with Queen Elizabeth 1 who always had lavender on hand for tea and other medicinal uses. Lavender is a more unusual ingredient in biscuits and cakes but can add a delicious tang to a sweet biscuit. Various recipes can be adapted to incorporate lavender flowers, but a plain, buttery shortbread recipe seems to work particularly well. Lavender jelly spread on brown bread or scones is also a delicious tea-time treat, or try lavender and rosemary or lavender and apple conserve. Experiment with the amount of lavender you use until you find the right level.

LAVENDER TEA

Infuse a tablespoon of dried lavender flowers in boiling water for about three to four minutes and then serve the tea with honey for a sweeter taste, or a slice of lemon for a more tangy flavour.

LAVENDER BISCUITS

*Cream 125 g (5 oz) butter with
100 g (4 oz) sugar and add 1
beaten egg. Mix in 1 tablespoon of
dried lavender flowers and 150 g
(6 oz) self-raising flour. Place the
mixture in small heaps on a greased
baking tray and bake at 170°C
(350°F, Gas 4) for about 15 to 20
minutes or until the biscuits are
golden brown in colour.*

INDEX

ACKNOWLEDGMENTS

The author *would like to thank* DAVID CHRISTIE *of Jersey Lavender Farm,
St Brelade, Jersey, Channel Islands,
for his helpful information and supplies of fresh lavender;
and* MANDY HOLMES *and* DIANA HATHERLY
for their sewing and cookery skills.

Dorling Kindersley *would like to thank* PATRICIA DEWHURST
*for kindly lending props for photography,
and* STEVE DOBSON *for his help with photography.*

Border illustrations *by Dorothy Tucker.*

41